THE FREUD ANNIVERSARY
LECTURE SERIES
THE NEW YORK PSYCHOANALYTIC
INSTITUTE

THE FREUD ANNIVERSARY LECTURE SERIES

The New York Psychoanalytic Institute

CURIOSITY

Herman Nunberg, M.D.

INTERNATIONAL UNIVERSITIES PRESS

New York

This work consists of an expanded version of
the lecture given at The New York Academy
of Medicine on May 17, 1960.

Contents

Curiosity

Mr. Chairman, Ladies and Gentlemen

For a long time I have wished to demonstrate, by using a case in treatment, how an analysis unfolds. However, when I set myself to work, I found that this is an almost impossible undertaking as the presentation of the full analysis of a case would require an excessive amount of time. Nevertheless, I should like you to take at least a brief look into the psychoanalytic workshop: I shall try to show, by means of a fragment of an analysis, how a theoretical understanding of certain problems gradually evolves. Even from such an abridged proceeding one can learn how complicated an analysis is, how intricate psychic processes are, and how cautious one should be in his theoretical conclusions.

The analysis of each case offers many problems; as I have to limit myself only to one, I have selected the problem of curiosity because it dominates the life of the patient I am going to present. We shall see that for the understanding of a single problem the patient's entire life must serve as a background. Even so, many questions will remain unanswered.

In the course of his investigations Freud learned, as he remarks, that psychic phenomena can best be studied in pathological exaggeration. For instance, as long as ego and superego are integrated, the individual is not aware of his conscience; only when there is a conflict and they are split does he become aware of the existence of his conscience.

For the observer, likewise, it is often difficult to conclude from the behavior of the so-called normal person that he has a conscience or superego, whereas he certainly can do so with much greater ease when he watches an individual in conflict, that is, in an abnormal state. When phenomena are pathologically exaggerated they can be seen better than when they are in the normal state of integration with other phenomena. Thus we hope from the investigation of the patient's main symptom, curiosity, to be able to reach some conclusions about the normal development and function of this phenomenon. Briefly, the purpose of this paper is twofold: to give an idea of analytic procedure as well as to show the metamorphosis and the meaning of curiosity.

Before I begin, I should like to state that I cannot offer new basic insights into a problem which has been treated extensively in psychoanalytic literature. In addition to Freud's fundamental work in the *Three Essays on the Theory of Sexuality* (1905), *Leonardo da Vinci and a Memory of his Childhood* (1910), and some other papers, there are quite a number of other psychoanalytic contributions to the same topic.

The extremely complex phenomenon of curiosity expresses itself in many ways, such as looking, listening, touching. Of course, in one instance one form of expression may prevail, in another a different one. Whenever I speak here of looking, touching, hearing, etc., I am referring to manifestations of curiosity. Through the gratification of curiosity one acquires a certain stock of knowledge, which may again lead to new problems and the formulation of new questions. Curiosity may therefore also be called an *urge for knowledge*.

Our patient suffered from the compulsion to ask questions and to look for answers. He had simple questions and answers as well as complicated ones. Some questions and answers were satisfactory to him and others were not. Both types of questions were accompanied by anxiety. When an answer was satisfactory, the anxiety disappeared; when it was unsatisfactory, the anxiety built up to panic. Among the variety of his questions was, for instance, the following: What is speaking? How does it take place? How does it start? Questions about the start, the beginning, overwhelmed him very often, in the most unexpected disguises. On one occasion he asked, "Do I say things which are original?" When I asked him to explain the meaning of the word "original," he answered promptly, "It means childbirth, how you are born." Upon my request for further clarification he said, "Do you not see, the word 'original' is 'origin' and that means 'beginning,' how the child is started; how it is born." Thus, without further analysis, it was evident that these questions contained in a disguised form the question of how man is born. Similarly, the question "how thoughts start" meant how a thought is born, and the questions about origin and formation of words had a similar meaning.

This type of question was accompanied by slight anxiety. Another type was coupled with somewhat greater anxiety which, however, could be checked by an answer that included the words, "to a certain degree." An example: "Do I love people?" Answer: "Everybody loves everybody to a certain degree." This answer was satisfactory to him; it is easy to see why: he evaded the issue by generalization and at the same time restricted the validity of the answer by adding the words, "to a certain degree." It was a kind of compromise in which one part of the sentence contradicted the other. In brief, the answer was ambivalent.

A third type of question looked as follows: "Are there times when you say things which have a regular top-surface-do-aspect?" Answer: "Everything a person does has a regular surface-do-aspect, unless he says something, to a degree." Neither the form of these questions nor that of the answers satisfied him, and the more he tried to change the formulations, the more complicated and nonsensical they became. Finally, he became confused, dizzy, nauseated, and the full attack of panic set in. It would last from a few days to four, five, or six months. During the attacks he had to stay home, secluded in his darkened bedroom, unable to go to work.

There is no doubt as to the diagnosis: this is an obsessional neurosis. We know then that we have to expect a regression of the libido to the anal-sadistic phase and a strict, overdemanding superego. I have published a short fragment of this case in my book, *Principles of Psychoanalysis* (1955, pp. 343-346). I reported there that the patient became aware of his first attack when he was sixteen years old. On his way home from school he had to ask himself when, precisely, the period of Renaissance began and when it ended. Of course, he could not find a satisfactory answer. When he spoke again about this attack, the following recollection came to his mind. One morning—he was about ten years old—his sister came down to the kitchen carrying a bundle. Asked what it contained, she gave no answer but ran outside and threw it into the garbage can. He followed her, took the bundle out, unwrapped it, and found a bloody cloth. Enormously embarrassed, he threw it back and never mentioned this incident again. Obviously, with one part of his ego he knew quite well that the bundle contained a sanitary napkin, but with another part he denied this knowledge to himself.

The question when the period of the Renaissance begins and when it ends thus means: when does the menstrual period begin and when does it end? Since the word "Re-naissance" means "rebirth," this question again deals with birth, the origin of man. Certainly, all of the patient's questions have a sexual background. Sexual curiosity plays, indeed, an important role in the normal life of children and adults, as well as in certain types of perversion and neurosis. To follow up the vicissitudes of curiosity, however, we must learn more about our patient's life.

He had an interesting relationship with his sister, who was four years his senior. Perhaps his earliest childhood recollection referred to the fact that she had almost bitten off his toe when he was about a year old. He did not remember the fact as such, nor did he remember when he heard about it for the first time, but he had the feeling that he had known of it all his life. During the analysis he asked his sister for more information about this incident. She confirmed his "recollection" and even asked him whether he still had the scar on his toe. Up to his sixth year the relationship between the two children was highly ambivalent. There was much fighting between them; when he complained, his mother would take his side and punish the sister.

He loved his mother passionately and was very attached to her. The father disapproved of this excessive attachment and endeavored to counterbalance it by teaching him how to wrestle, to box, swim, etc. When, in spite of his efforts, he saw no change in the boy, the father became impatient, chided the child for behaving like a girl, called him a sissy and threatened "to cut him off his mother's apron strings." The harder the father tried to separate him from his mother, the more he clung to her. In order to stimulate his masculinity, his father sent him to summer camp as soon as he was six years old. Immediately after his return home, the father took the whole family to Europe. The children were placed in two separate though neighboring schools and the parents left. After a year had elapsed, they took the children back home.

This experience seems to have been the turning point in the patient's life. Before the trip he loved his mother and was ambivalent to the sister. This changed while he was abroad. It appeared as if he had lost his love for the mother and had begun to love the sister. When he returned home, he felt like a stranger in the family, talked neither to mother nor father, but became increasingly close to the sister. Obviously, the love for the sister had been substituted for the love of his mother.

When he was about nine years old, or perhaps somewhat younger, anxiety dreams about a man with a gun and a *flashlight* trying to force himself into his room began to disturb his sleep. Awakened by anxiety, he would ask his sister in the adjoining room to let him come into her bed. When she consented, he slipped quietly into her room. Before settling in her bed, however, he had to perform a certain ritual: he had to lie down, his head at her feet and his back toward hers, while no part of his body was allowed to touch hers. When I asked him whether he had always succeeded in keeping a proper distance between himself and the sister, he remarked that he had no sexual thoughts about or desires for her (as if he understood what my question implied). Yet he developed a kind of negative reaction. That is, it became his habit to be very careful not to touch her; in fact, he avoided coming close to her. This avoidance of touching persisted into adulthood, became generalized, and extended even to his own children. He feared that by touching he might harm them.

The clandestine relation with his sister continued until his sixteenth year. When he was fifteen the family moved to an apartment where he shared the bedroom with his sister. They

[15]

had twin beds like a married couple, but since the beds were separated by a bed table, there was less chance of touching than of seeing one another. He took great pains *not to see her nude* and *not to be seen nude by her*, which was perhaps more important to him. *On the other hand, he looked and peeped with great pleasure* when it did not concern her. For instance, when girl friends came to visit her and stayed overnight (on such occasions he would sleep in the living room), he peeped through the keyhole trying to get a glimpse of them while they were *dressing* or *undressing*, and he had sexual desires for and dreams about them.

The avoidance of both looking and touching thus was a reaction formation against the urges to do so. All of his defenses, however, including the repression proper, could not withstand the increased demands of the libido in puberty. Especially in the last year in which he shared the bedroom with his sister, he was disturbed by the ever-growing intensity of his sexual urges as well as by wet dreams, the contents of which he could not remember. Yet in spite of his sexual hypersensitivity, he did not masturbate until his sister was married and left the parental home. He was then sixteen years old. Whenever he would meet her afterwards, he was embarrassed and unable to talk to her, just as he had been unable to talk to his mother after his disappointment in her in Europe. Obviously he felt that she had deserted him, just as the mother had done.

Until her marriage the sister was sexually taboo to him. Afterwards, he would speculate about her sexual relations with her husband and ask himself many questions about her sexuality. But there was no satisfactory answer. So he would walk the streets and look at women, asking himself how their sex organs looked and whether they had sexual relations. He went to movies, to burlesque shows, strip-tease performances; he would peep into neighbors' windows, and the like.

It is obvious that he could control his sexual feelings as long as he shared the room with his sister, but as soon as he was left to himself, the repressed sexuality exploded and appeared first as a perversion in the shape of sexual curiosity. In other words, *instead of choosing another sexual object after the loss of the sister, he made a regression to sexual curiosity.*

When in this period he peeped into a neighbor's window and saw a nude man, he was so impressed by the size of his penis that in great distress he asked himself repeatedly, "How can a man do that to a woman?"—meaning how can a man be so cruel to a woman. In truth he wanted to know whether his father was as cruel to his mother.

He reacted to the session in which he related this experience with the following dream. He was in bed with his wife making love to her but had the feeling that his son was watching him. When he turned toward the child's bed, he saw him lying quietly there but he was not sure whether the boy was actually asleep or only pretending to be. His son's attitude seemed familiar to him; it reminded him that he himself had often pretended to sleep when sleeping was expected of him. Then he remembered his own crib in his parents' bedroom and the noises which would wake him up at night. One could sense the unformulated questions of the little child, questions which the mature man tried to answer in his neurosis (Nunberg, 1955, p. 346).

In this dream the patient projects himself into his son, at the same time identifying himself with his father. The son, who represents the patient, watches him as he himself had once watched his father. Watching means looking with the purpose of finding out something, often without a clear formulation of a question. A child cannot ask questions before he can talk.

Yet he is able to express feelings and emotions such as joy, pain, surprise, astonishment, curiosity by the intonation of his voice, by a gesture, by the posture of his body. The child in the dream did not talk, he lifted his head and looked at the father. Watching the father, looking at that early age, may dramatize a question, as if the child were asking, "What are you doing?"

We know that all children are sexually curious, but also that they give up this curiosity in the course of development. Our patient, however, seems to have retained much of it and satisfied it in a more or less disguised form in many ways, masturbatory fantasies among them. As indicated before, he did not masturbate until his sister was married. Then he began to masturbate with the following fantasy. He put a woman, most frequently his father's secretary, on an operating table, tied her and made her helpless, then undressed her and looked at her until he became sexually very excited. In this fantasy, looking is a sadistic act. As a mature man he would ask himself, while in the act of copulating with his wife, whether he derived more pleasure from looking, touching, and squeezing her than from intercourse. This man, who treated his wife with utmost consideration, had to have her face lighted during copulation so that he could see whether she showed signs of pain. His curiosity thus was mixed with a great deal of sadism.

His scoptophilic, sadistic fantasy persisted for a long time without change. Before that, in pre-puberty, he had another fantasy which was of rather a masochistic nature. In order to understand the relationship between the two, we have to go back to the period following his return from Europe.

We remember his father's disapproval of the boy's excessive attachment to the mother and of his femininity, and I have reported that he separated his son from her for a year. After the family had returned home, the boy made up his mind to become a real man. He took up a variety of sports, such as boxing, football, etc., and in the course of time became a first-rate athlete, a champion. Yet he failed to impress his father with the numerous trophies he brought home. He was not interested in girls, except for his sister, but formed many friend-ships with boys. His best friend, Timmy, was also an excellent athlete. Timmy was not a strong boy of athletic build; he was rather girl-ish, slim, weak-looking, but agile and alert. Their friendship was so great that they never played against one another in any competitive game, but always together on one team against others. They also played fantasy games together, one of which they called the *Pirate game*. They were then between nine and eleven years old. The game was played in the following way: they would lie on their stomachs on separate beds; our patient would be the leader, calling out each step of the game in the manner of a radio announcer. He would say, for instance, "Now we climb up the pirate ship; now we draw our swords and fight the pirates." Suddenly they would notice that the pirates were women, not men as they had expected, whereupon they would stop fighting and surrender. It was a matter of honor to him not to fight women. The female pirates captured him, tied him to the ship's mast and made him helpless; then they undressed the upper part of his body down to the waist, looked at him, and asked where the treasure was hidden. He did not betray the secret and saw himself as a hero. When he refused to answer, the female leader gave the order to whip him. When he still remained silent, she ordered that his trousers be taken off. At this point he became very excited sexually and broke off the fantasy game.

This fantasy was the opposite of the postpubertal fantasy. In the latter he was active, sadistic, *looking* at the helpless nude woman; in the former he was passive, masochistic, undressed and *looked at by the woman*. In both fantasies the sexual excitement became overwhelming; in the later one by *searchingly looking* at a woman, in the earlier one by *being asked questions and looked at by a woman*.

The content of the pirate fantasy was composed of real and psychic elements.[1] The concept of the pirate ships and hidden treasures stems, of course, from stories and moving pictures. The costumes in which the pirate women were dressed stemmed from experiences in the attic of the parental home. From early childhood on the patient and his sister used to play there with costumes they had found in a chest. She would dress in such a costume and dance before him to his great delight. The pirate

---

[1] Fantasies are reactions of the ego to the urges of the id, on the one hand, and to the demands of reality, on the other; they are a compromise between the two. All small children have fantasies which may be considered unconscious at that age. In latency they become conscious in a distorted form; we may say that they are preconscious. All fantasies undergo changes in the course of development; they may be repressed and are then transformed into character traits; they may be dormant, that is inactive, and take no effect on the behavior of the individual. Under certain circumstances they may become active, that is, charged with energy, and then they influence the individual's creativity or lead to perversions or neuroses.

[22]

leader, dressed in this costume, thus represented (in one layer) the sister. We remember: when he would come to her bed at night, frightened by a dream, he denied himself the pleasure of touching or looking at her, because, he said, he was afraid he might harm her. In the pirate game he took on a passive role, as if he were saying, "Not I am curious about the pirate woman (my sister), not I want to touch her or to see her nude, but she wants to touch (to beat) me and to look at me." The whip of the pirate women reminded him of the cat-o'-nine-tails hanging from the kitchen wall throughout his childhood. Whenever he was naughty, his mother would threaten to whip him, but never did. Finally, he wished she would do it.

As the whip is a well-known penis symbol, we may assume that the patient equipped the pirate woman, the sister and mother substitute, with a symbolic penis. If this interpretation is correct, we have here a classic example of the concept of the woman with a penis, found so often in both men and women. His friend Timmy, a male, reminded him of his sister in many ways, such as in his slight build and the rhythm of his movements. The fact that he re-fused to play against him in competitive games was even more convincing. He said he could not beat his best friend. When he fought with his sister and in the end hit her, his father would get very angry and warn him sternly not to do that again, stressing that one does not do that to a girl. In the pirate game he could not fight the pirates as soon as he discovered that they were women, and he had to be as considerate of Timmy as he was expected to be of his sister.[2]

The pirate fantasy during which each boy was masturbating for himself was in fact a mutual masturbation fantasy. If we add that the patient many times felt the urge to jump upon his friend and to rub his penis against Timmy's, we recognize that the wish for sexual gratification was displaced from the sister onto the friend. If it is true that Timmy represented her, then she was a bisexual creature in his eyes—a male and a female.

The house to which the family moved when the patient was fifteen years old was a great distance from the old residence. It made him very unhappy that he could no longer see his friend daily. Moreover, as Timmy's friendship

[2] A certain type of homosexual retains in his object choice some of the features characteristic of his repressed first sexual object. The patient had first repressed the love of which his mother was the object by substituting the sister for her; then he exchanged the latter for Timmy.

cooled off gradually, he felt deserted, depressed, and lonesome. The frustration of the homosexual friendship may well have contributed more to his final breakdown than his sister's marriage. Frustrated homosexuality seems to have been a factor in his regression to infantile, aggressive sexual curiosity.

Now we have to ask ourselves how and when he acquired the idea that his sister had a penis—an idea which contradicted the perception of his sense organs. It was difficult to establish the exact time at which he first noticed the difference between his own and her sexual organs. It is certain, however, that he was very young when he first asked his mother questions about the difference, long before the trip to Europe. He did not believe her answers and found one for himself: the father had cut off the sister's penis. This was consistent with his ideas about sexual intercourse in which the woman is hurt and injured by the man. However, he very soon became dissatisfied with this solution, and became anxious and restless. After much doubting and brooding, he came to the conclusion that the sister had a penis but that it was hidden high up in the abdomen, *for protection.*

It is interesting to note that the painful perception of the difference between himself and his sister stimulated his curiosity. The explanation which he gave himself first provoked restlessness and anxiety. This anxiety, which can only be interpreted as castration anxiety, in turn stimulated other questions, speculations and answers, which seemed to be aimed at providing reassurance and comfort. With the reassuring answer that the sister, a woman, has a penis, his anxiety disappeared for a while. Even though his answers were incorrect, the questions, speculations, and quasi-logical deductions still are a sign of intellectual activity; indeed, not infrequently do painful experiences give the impetus to intellectual and artistic creativity.[3]

Let us now continue with the analysis of the

[3] I see in this phenomenon, which evolves at the very beginning of the latency period, a parallel to the intellectualization in puberty as observed by Anna Freud (1936). According to her, the intensified intellectual activity of the adolescent helps him in mastering the increased pressure of the libido in puberty. It seems that in our case—and in others which I have observed—castration fear on the one hand supports the inhibitions demanded by upbringing, and checks infantile curiosity with all its consequences, while on the other hand it stimulates the development of mental activity. This is another manifestation of the importance of the castration complex. As Freud has said, not only can it influence the mental development (as it does in our case), but also the character development and is the factor which is decisive in regard to an individual's health or illness. The castration complex is ubiquitous and seems to be inherited, like the oedipus complex. External events and traumata, like those castration threats on the part of the patient's mother, may, at the most, modify or enforce the castration complex, but they do not create it.

pirate fantasy. Two events occurred immediately before its emergence. Under our patient's leadership, a group of boys in school ganged up on one of their schoolmates and tried to undress him; he was a frail, blond, girlish-looking boy. When our patient noticed how desperately he defended himself and how he suffered, he felt pity for him and guilt and ceased to participate in the assault. Shortly thereafter a group of strange boys accosted him and asked whether he had a sister. Upon his affirmative answer they demanded her address. Sensing that something was wrong, he gave them false information. After they had left, Timmy told him that they belonged to a gang of boys who kidnapped girls, tied, undressed, and looked at them. Although he condemned the supposed activities of these boys, he felt a strange sexual excitement. It was soon after this that the pirate games with Timmy began.

In these games he carried out the exact opposite of what the gang of boys were supposed to do to the girls and what he himself had wanted to do with the girlish boy in school. These boys were sadistic and looked at nude girls; in the pirate game the girls were sadistic, undressed him and looked at him. The idea of active looking changed into passive feelings of being looked at. It was only years later that he permitted himself to do in his fantasy with the secretary what he had been afraid the boys were going to do to his sister and what he had wanted to do to the sister substitute. However, the appearance of the gang immediately after the assault on the girlish boy seems to have weakened his ego in his effort to repress his desire for the sister. Yet he did not succumb to the temptation, but reinforced the repression by reversing the desire to look and to touch into its opposite, that is, into being looked at and beaten in the pirate fantasy.

When he boarded the pirate ship in this game, he expected to find men there and was prepared to fight them, but instead found women dressed like men. Our patient had numerous anxiety dreams in which he was savagely fighting with a man. There is no doubt that the man represented his father. He was never afraid of his mother or of the pirate woman in the fantasy, but of the father. It is, therefore, likely that he substituted the mother for the father at the last moment, as if he were saying that the pirate woman was less dangerous than the pirate man. Thus the pirate fantasy was a bisexual fantasy: heterosexual in so far as it was conscious, homosexual as well as dangerous in so far as it was unconscious.

We indicated a moment ago that the secretary fantasy was a straight reversal of the pirate fantasy of his prepuberty years, in which he was passive and masochistic. Moreover, in the secretary fantasy the woman is entirely a woman, not a bisexual being. This fantasy represents, in a sense, a progress from passivity and homosexuality to activity and heterosexuality. He stressed many times that he felt the greatest sexual excitement when, in the secretary fantasy, he overpowered the woman and tore the blouse from her body, just as in the pirate fantasy he felt the greatest excitement when the woman threatened to remove his trousers. Obviously, looking, which was in his mind the same as investigating, became alternately a sadistic and a masochistic act.

The repressed wish to look, to investigate, to be active and aggressive appeared, as mentioned before, in the pirate fantasy as its counterpart, the fear of being looked at and examined. (The intensity of his fear of being looked at can be judged from the fact that after years of married life and fatherhood he was unable to undress in his wife's presence.) It may thus be assumed that the pirate fantasy on the whole was a defense

[29]

against his aggression toward the sister, the aggression which became conscious as a sexual urge aimed at a sister (mother) substitute in the secretary fantasy.

The patient himself rationalized his fear of being looked at with a fear of being laughed at. The latter stemmed, in fact, from his sister's laughing at him and pointing her finger at his penis when she saw him naked as a little boy. He remembered an incident in his fifth year when she came into the bathroom while he was standing nude in the bathtub. He became frightened because the way she looked at him made him feel that she would take his penis away from him, that she might castrate him by looking. His fear of being seen nude expresses both fear of castration and fear of exposing his "inferior" penis.

When in the fantasy the pirate woman gave the order to beat him, he had the mental picture of his own back covered with red, bloody streaks. Evidently he split himself and saw or hallucinated his own back in projection in the external world. It reminded him of an experience he had had when he was four years old. A lady took him and her little son to a bathhouse on the beach. She asked the children to turn to the wall and not to look while she was undressing, but our patient turned around and looked at her. She caught him at it and said sternly, "No peeking!" However, he had had enough time to catch a glimpse of her back, which seemed to him covered with red, bloody streaks, as if after a whipping. Thus he identified in the pirate fantasy with a beaten, injured woman. In one layer the fantasy of being beaten by a woman means the fulfillment of his old wish to be whipped by his mother. But we have interpreted the pirate woman as a woman with a penis, that is, a man. If we take into account that a fantasy, like a dream, is always over-determined, we may say that he is beaten not only by a woman but also by a man. If we fur-ther remember that in his imagination the father beat and injured the mother at night, we must assume that, in the deepest layer of his fantasy, the patient identified with his mother as beaten by his father. Being afraid to expose his genitals as well as being afraid to look at a woman's stems from the same source, the castra-tion complex. In the first case he fears castra-tion; in the second he is afraid to look at a human being who has no penis.

Yet there was a time when he was not afraid to be exposed and looked at. About half a year after the beginning of his analysis his sister told

him something which she thought might be use-
ful in his treatment. When he was two and a
half years old a maid played with him sexually
on the bathroom floor. He could not remember
any event of that kind, but a picture came to
his mind of himself lying on the bathroom floor
and the maid or nurse kissing his penis. Sub-
sequently, whenever he thought of his sister's
story, he saw the nurse or maid kissing his penis;
in the end he began to believe that the picture
was not an imagination but the recollection of a
real event.[4] Since it was difficult to ascertain
what really happened, I consented to his asking
his sister about the details. The sister, who was
six and a half years old at the time when the
event supposedly took place, confirmed his "hallucinated" recollection and added that their
mother dismissed the maid immediately when
she came home and learned what had happened.
The mother gave a different version. She remembered that upon coming home one after-
noon she found the *nursemaid* drunk on the
floor before the bathroom and the boy holding
his penis and crying because he could not uri-
nate. She dismissed the maid on the spot and

4 It happens frequently that what emerges first as a vision or
hallucination in the course of an analysis proves to be a real
recollection.

[32]

took the child to the doctor. He informed her
that the boy's penis was infected and advised to
keep it clean. The mother, who had a compul-
sive character, took the doctor's advice very
seriously, washed the boy's penis often, and
warned him constantly not to touch it and to
keep it clean. Should he fail to obey, she threatened, his penis would get *infected* again and
fall off. Under this pressure he washed his penis
carefully indeed, probably masturbating at the
same time. Later he became very neat and clean,
washed his hands exceedingly often, perhaps
once every hour, though never to such an extent that it would interfere with his daily activities in business and elsewhere. Only after the
discussion of his anality, he revealed that in the
beginning of his analysis he had always omitted
to express the thought, "and not to be infected," when he was talking about "how a man
can put his penis in the dirty, messy genitalium
of a woman." His anality which, as will be seen
later, played also a considerable part in his
infantile birth and pregnancy theories, thus
contributed to the formation of certain character traits such as his neatness and overcleanli-
ness, and to the development of his disgust at
the female genitalia (Freud, 1908). In addition,
it stimulated the formation of the castration

[33]

complex in the form of fear of *infection* by the woman.

Let us now return to the bathroom scene. How is the difference between the versions of sister and mother to be understood? It is likely that the sister gave an account of what she saw and the mother one of her own experience. Assuming that the sister's report is correct, how is it possible that she remembered all the details unless she was present and participated in the boy's seduction, or even stimulated him herself, later projecting this onto the nursemaid? This seems quite probable if we take into account that she was very aggressive, a tomboy, that she had actually almost bitten off his toe when he was about a year old, and that, on the other hand, the patient hardly remembered nurse or maid but seemed to remember the kissing of his penis. The mother's version is easy to explain. She may well have come home another time and found the drunken maid and the crying boy outside the bathroom. In the patient's feeling, however, the bathroom scene and the scene in the doctor's office were so closely linked that they almost constituted a unity. Perhaps we can understand this if we consider that both had a common denominator: gratification in the state of passivity. In the doctor's office he was lying

[34]

on his back on a couch or table while the doctor was doing something to him under a strong light and two women in white, the mother and the nurse, were at his sides *looking at him.* In the bathroom scene he was lying on his back while two women (nurse and/or[5] maid) were kissing his penis.

He had no other association to the scene in the doctor's office except one which would always come to his mind whenever he thought of this scene, namely, a mental picture of himself playing some athletic competitive game, such as baseball, while thousands of people were watching and admiring him, and he was feeling a hero. He retained this fantasy unchanged into adulthood. He had it every night before falling asleep; it was like "a mother's good-night kiss," he remarked once. He produced this fantasy also when he would wake up at night and could not go back to sleep; it worked like a hypnotic.

The gratification of being looked at and admired is certainly a narcissistic one; the technique for achieving this goal, that is, showing oneself, is called exhibitionism. It is a counterpart to voyeurism or scoptophilia and, perhaps in a broader sense, to curiosity. Scoptophilia as

[5] In the unconscious "or" often means "and."

well as the desire to touch, listen, taste, or smell, can be gratified by the stimulation of an erotogenic zone, such as the eye, the skin, the ear. Exhibitionism cannot be satisfied by stimulation of an erotogenic zone, since there is none for the exhibitionistic drive. It can be satisfied only by identification with the onlooker, that is, with an object of the external world. When the patient was gratified by the fantasy of a woman looking at him in the pirate game or by the fantasy of a crowd watching him playing some athletic game, he regressed to the time of the scene in the doctor's office, to the narcissistic gratification in exhibitionism, that is, to the early times when mother looked at him with admiring affection.

The scene in the doctor's office has still another connotation: he was struck by the fact that the doctor used a glaring light for examining his penis. Repeatedly he called my attention to this light, which he called a flashlight, as if he were trying to tell me that this was something very important. Actually, a flashlight played an important role during his childhood until puberty. As mentioned before, he had a repetitive dream in which he lay in bed in his room, his face turned to the wall, when suddenly he heard heavy steps of a man coming up

[36]

the stairs and approaching his room. He turned around in his bed in order to see who was coming and was hit by a strong flashlight when the man opened the door and tried to find him. He awoke with anxiety and went to his sister's bed.

So the scene in the doctor's office seems to have branched out in several directions: (1) fear of genital infection through contact with a woman; (2) reaction formations against anal stimuli and wishes; (3) fear of castration by the father when found by him with a flashlight, i.e., when being watched by him; and (4) narcissistic gratification derived from the feeling of being watched by others. This last ramification is of great importance for it throws into relief that showing oneself nude not only gives narcissistic pleasure but, as an attempt to seduce the onlooker, may also become a danger. In other words, to be admired by mother gives pleasure, while to be admired by a man may be dangerous.

It may appear that all this has not much to do with the problem of curiosity; the following material will lead us slowly back to this problem. We return to our patient's trip to Europe.

On the boat he had many anxiety dreams of which he remembered only one: somebody throws him overboard into the ocean; he sees the ship moving away from him, farther and farther; he tries to swim, to hold on to something, perhaps a board, but there is no help, the waves are closing in and he feels desperate, alone, helpless. He woke up in panic.

Knowing the background of this dream, one had no great difficulty in understanding it, at least to a certain point. On the ship the boy had been told of the impending separation from his family, and he was full of worries and fears. Since a ship very often symbolizes a woman, we may interpret the boat in the dream as a symbol of his mother. Being thrown into the ocean means, then, being separated from her. The father was the only person who could perform this brutal act. We recall that the father considered him effeminate and too much attached to his mother and had threatened "to cut him off her apron strings"; therefore we must conclude that the dreamer was afraid to be separated from his mother by castration. If this interpretation is correct, we understand the panic which woke him up, a panic which frustrated the wish-fulfillment tendency of the dream. Translated into conscious language the dream says: I submit to my father's wish to separate from my mother, but if it implies castration I will not do so.

[38]

Thus the attempt to please the father is frustrated by castration fear.

This dream is overdetermined, as are all dreams. The patient's mind was occupied with many thoughts on that trip, one of which pursued him with particular persistence. It concerned the Count of Monte Cristo, the hero of Alexandre Dumas's novel.[6] He felt compelled to visualize over and over again the episode in which the hero was captured by his enemies, dragged into prison, sewn into a sack, and thrown into a canal, a sewer. The Count cuts the sack open from within, slips out of it and swims from the sewer into open, clean water, thus escaping from the dreadful and disgusting prison.

The fascination which this episode had for our patient is easily accounted for by one of his birth theories. Supplementing his old belief that the father was beating and injuring the mother in sexual intercourse, he imagined at a later stage of development that the child is born when the doctor cuts the mother's abdomen open with a knife. Certainly the doctor is a

6 It was difficult to ascertain how a child of his age came to be acquainted with this novel. One of his aunts who read innumerable stories to him throughout his childhood may have chosen that one, too.

substitute for the father and the knife a symbol of his penis. In the novel there is no doctor who cuts the sack, but it is the prisoner himself who does it. Obviously, the child identified with the Count, who is his own obstetrician; in other words, he gave birth to himself, he was reborn. Besides the fact that all birth fantasies are both active and passive, our patient himself stressed many times that thinking about the baby in the mother's body, he always saw and felt himself as the baby. The cesspool in which the hero is swimming struck again a familiar note. The boy's idea was that the unborn baby is swimming in urine and feces inside the mother, as if he knew the old proverb, *"Inter faeces et urinam nascimur."* He would speculate how a child could live there, see in the dark, breathe, eat, and get out of there. One gains the impression that he had endeavored to look inside the mother, to penetrate into her, as in later years he tried to penetrate secrets by peeping. We find offshoots of this problem in the questions he asked himself in later years, such as, "Do I inhale or exhale when I am hitting the [golf]ball?" To which he would answer, "You neither inhale nor exhale by the mouth; you keep it shut; you suck in the air by your anus."

None of these thoughts, questions, and fantasies appear in the manifest dream, but they are contained in the latent dream thoughts; they are represented by the Count, who serves as an intermediary link. (We know that omissions in the dream serve the purpose of disguise.) All the latent dream thoughts attached to the Count lead us to understand that the dream expresses not only separation and castration wishes but also anal-sadistic birth ideas. What separates the baby more radically from the mother than birth, and what causes more anxiety? The fact that the manifest dream does not contain the slightest hint of anal or sadistic urges is sufficient to show how deeply repressed these anal urges were even at that time.

The multiple determinants of the manifest dream expressed themselves in still another detail which at first seemed insignificant. The dreamer was trying to catch a board "to hold on to" in the ocean. A piece of wood, a board, symbolizes the mother or her breast; hence we may assume that the dreamer was trying to attach himself to the mother's breast in order to undo the separation. And in reality, the woman's breasts played an enormous role in the patient's love life; they held an almost fetishlike fascination for him. Until the age of four or five he was a passionate thumb sucker. He remembered clearly that when he masturbated while sucking his finger, he had a mental picture of his mother's breasts with him in bed. In her effort to wean him from thumb sucking, she used to threaten that his finger would be sucked in and disappear in his stomach. When he compared the two thumbs, it seemed to him that his pleasure-finger was really getting smaller, and he became afraid of losing it. When she warned him against eating fruit pits, another fear was added: he became afraid that an apple tree, an orange tree, or another fruit tree might grow in his stomach. There is no doubt that the thumb symbolically played the role of breasts as well as that of penis, while the fruits growing in his stomach symbolized children.[7] He had so many pregnancy and birth fantasies that it is almost impossible to enumerate them. Even the swimming in the ocean of the manifest dream represents a pregnancy fantasy demonstrating the dangers of birth. For water in a dream has always a symbolic relation to the mother's womb, pregnancy and birth. Derivatives of these fantasies manifested themselves, as we have seen, in innocuous questions, like the one

[7] About the transition from breast to penis, see Freud's *Leonardo da Vinci* (1910); and about the symbolic meaning of the thumb, see Rank's (1913) analyses of Grimm's fairy tales.

[42]

about originality, the origin of speech and thinking, the Renaissance period, etc. From early childhood until the time of his illness he was almost wholly absorbed with the problems of birth; and in his illness these problems constituted at least one component of each of his questions.

It is difficult to say when he first began to ask these questions. The analysis of his dream about the primal scene led us to the conclusion that he already had questions in very early childhood, even though he was not yet able to express them in words. He remembered that he asked mother and sister questions about birth even before he was four years old and that either he received the usual evasive answers or was met with laughter. Of course he rejected the answers; he formed his own theory, namely, that the doctor cuts the baby out of the mother's body. Evidently this theory was an extension of his earlier ideas about father injuring mother at night. So deeply ingrained was this theory that later in life whenever his wife was in labor he would become panicky and enormously afraid that mother and child would be killed.

Freud suggests that curiosity may be stimulated by a birth in the family, but no birth occurred in the patient's environment during

[43]

his early childhood. Freud further suggests that death may have the same effect, for death is associated with life, thus with birth. In fact, the patient's grandmother died when he was three years old. A day before her death he was taken to her sickroom and became terribly frightened at the sight of her enormously distended abdomen. When he saw the next day that his mother was very unhappy and was told that the grandmother had died, he thought that her stomach had burst. In the analysis he made a connection between her death and the enemas which his mother used to give him in his childhood. She would urge him to hold the water in his "stomach," and he would try to obey her; but when the pains became very strong he became afraid that his stomach would burst. When his mother did not permit him to flush the toilet because she wished to check his evacuation, he would ask himself whether she was looking for a baby he had produced. There is no doubt that he established a connection between his grandmother's distended belly and his anal-birth fantasies. However, it was difficult to decide whether he had already made this connection at the age of three years, at the time of her death, or made it later, and perhaps in the analysis projected his birth fantasies into the distant past. Although it was not yet possible to ascertain exactly when the child began to think about childbirth, it seemed clear that these problems emerged spontaneously when he was less than three years old.

In view of the complexity of psychic processes and of the fact that they are interwoven, let us now turn our attention again to the relationship between orality and looking which was expressed, for example, in the entanglement of the bathroom scene and the doctor's-office scene. This relationship became very clear in a particular transference situation.

When the patient's attacks had disappeared and he felt cured, the analysis was discontinued for the time being. It is well known that improvement is often used as a resistance which stalls for long periods a profitable continuation of the analysis. In such cases I have found it better to dismiss the patient in the certainty that he will return after some time. In fact, after eight months a slight new attack brought the patient back to treatment.

I have pointed out elsewhere (1925a) that recovery from illness means to the patient something different from what it means to the doctor, even though on the conscious level it seems to have the same meaning for both: to cure and to be cured. In the unconscious, however, it frequently implies to the patient the ability to enjoy the same gratification as in illness, but without inhibitions. This is, of course, a handicap for the treatment right at the beginning of the analysis. The sooner the analyst uncovers the specific meaning of the unconscious wish for recovery in each case, the easier the analysis will be. However, it is not always possible to detect the full extent of this meaning at the beginning of treatment, since the wish has different aspects on different levels. In the course of treatment the wish for recovery is absorbed and replaced by the transference.

Prior to the analysis with me the patient was in treatment with a psychotherapist. That treatment consisted in a sort of question-and-answer game. The patient asked questions and the doctor replied. When the patient saw after some time that he was making no progress he left this therapist. When he came to me he tried to play the same game. When he realized that I would not collaborate he gave me to understand that he did not believe in analysis. A while later, he expressed the conviction that he could not be cured at all, neither by his first doctor nor by me. Nevertheless, in spite of all his resistances he stayed in analysis and came regularly every day.

After his confession he began to associate and to provide enough material to enable me to make some interpretations. Soon, however, I saw that he did not accept them. Of course, I looked for signs of transference. He was very correct with me, friendly but without emotion; he was reserved, cool, as if he had erected a wall between us.

In this attitude toward me I saw a repetition of his attitude toward his mother after his return from Europe, when he began to ignore her and not to talk to her. He himself said that he felt at that time as if a wall were separating them. Just as the confession of his distrust in analysis did not change much, so it was that my explanation of his behavior toward me, by relating it to his attitude toward his mother, also produced little change. However, it brought out material from which I learned that he was unable to accept literally anything from his father, not even gifts for his children which at times would have been substantial. Under these circumstances it was as puzzling that he had forced his father to take him into his business as it was that he came regularly for his analysis while refusing to accept any interpretation. The father had not wanted him to join the business; he would have preferred that the son continue his studies. Nevertheless, the patient left college and persuaded the father that his business was the only suitable place of work for him. Once there, he opposed his father constantly and did not accept his guidance.[8]

The patient wanted from me direct answers to his questions; we may thus assume that his questions during the attacks were unconsciously addressed to his father, from whom he had also wanted direct answers, that is, sexual enlightenment. Most boys wish their fathers to introduce them to the mysteries of sex, i.e., they wish their

[8] Freud remarks that the refusal to accept anything from one's father implies the wish to reject his influence, the wish not to be his son. In my monograph on bisexuality and circumcision (1947) I dealt with rejection of and submission to the father's wish. The rejection was explained by the fear of being castrated by the father and thus transformed into a woman, the submission to the father's will by acceptance of the feminine, *passive* role. If we yield to our inclination for generalization, we may say that emotional acceptance of the analyst's interpretation means to the patient acceptance of the feminine, passive role—a danger. The refusal to accept interpretations plays a great role in the treatment and is both result and major source of resistances. This is true of women as well as of men. Freud has said several times that an analysis may have been carried out quite correctly, and yet the patient may not change. It is then left to the patient whether he is going to accept the interpretations—that means whether he will submit to the analyst's influence. This point of view leads to a comparison between psychoanalytic therapy and hypnosis. See Freud, *Group Psychology and Analysis of the Ego* (1921), and Nunberg, "Transference and Reality" (1951).

[48]

fathers would teach them how sexual intercourse is performed and how children are made,
which amounts to the wish for participation in
these mysteries. Our patient asked his mother
sexual questions and felt her answers to be unsatisfactory; he asked his sister, and she laughed
at him; he wanted to ask his father but was too
afraid of him. Why was he more afraid to put
these questions to father than to mother or sister? As we know, he reacted to his sexual questions with fantasies in which his father played
a prominent and unfavorable role. Unconsciously, our patient had a strong homosexual
attachment to him; the analysis of the attack
that brought him back into treatment was almost entirely taken up by this topic.

The circumstances under which this attack
occurred were the following. He was free of
symptoms, felt happy as never before, was gain-
ing weight, and was altogether satisfied with the
results of his analysis. He was very grateful,
thought often of me, and had the wish to visit
and thank me, but never found time to do so.
Then it happened that he wanted to go to a
party with his wife. She telephoned a woman
friend in order to make arrangements for going
there together. He overheard the conversation,
in the course of which the friend asked how

[49]

they would come home, since the men were usually drunk at the end of such a party. His wife replied that he could drive them back, since he never became intoxicated, regardless of how much liquor he drank. The woman at the other end of the wire said that she would still watch him closely when he was drinking. He asked his wife to repeat what her friend had said and as soon as he fully understood, he became restless and a question forced itself upon his mind. He tried to suppress it but could not.

This was the question: "Are there times when you tell a story and are there times when you are telling things which are not stories?" Answer: "Everything that you say is a story to a degree." This was followed by other questions and answers, which ended in anxiety.

We have to ask ourselves first: why did overhearing the telephone conversation between his wife and her friend provoke an attack; and second, what is the connection between this conversation and the questions about stories?

In reference to the telephone conversation he reminded me that during his analysis he had often had the feeling that he was talking to me over the phone; he was talking to me but could not see me. This made him feel uneasy.

Evidently he identified the woman at the other end of the telephone line with me. He complained often that he felt as if undressed, nude, when he had the impression that I was looking at him. We remember: he was afraid of being looked at and investigated. But what has the fear of being watched while drinking to do with the questions about stories?

To him analysis meant telling stories, and stories meant fairy stories—lies. Never, he said, had he lied in the analysis; however, he said he had kept one thing from me, and that was the topic of homosexuality and fellatio between men. This topic, and particularly oral relations with men, was so repulsive to him that he could not even think about it. Therefore, he added, he had avoided talking about it to me. (That is not correct; in fact, he had discussed this problem, but obviously repressed it again.)

Now we have perhaps found a reason for his failure to visit me in spite of his wish to do so. We can even understand how this is connected with his questions about stories, at least to some extent: he was afraid to confess the truth about his oral homosexual fantasies in relation to me, his analyst. He was, of course, unaware of that when the attack set in, but instead was afraid of the woman who would watch him drinking.

[51]

This woman in the role of a critical observer reminded him very much of his mother. The latter would inspect his ears, mouth, hands, even his excrements, and that at a time when he was no longer a little child. She would keep her watchful eye on him even at the dinner table. He used to drink much water, of which she disapproved, urging him to drink milk instead. He liked milk but could not take it without adding another flavor, such as coffee or cocoa. Up to maturity he had imagined that there was always milk in a woman's breasts, and that one had only to put one's mouth to her nipples for milk to flow in abundance. As a child he compared mother's nipples to the cow's teats and wondered why these were so long and the nipples so small. He asked himself also why mother had breasts and father had not. After much speculation he came to the conclusion that breasts are a kind of penis displaced from below upward.

The following illustrates how deeply set such ideas were in his unconscious and how they influenced the adult's behavior. While in treatment he went to see his mother once and reported afterward that his improvement was so great that he felt free in her presence and was even able to look at her without embarrassment as she came out of her bedroom in a nightgown. However, he was surprised by what followed. At about that time she sold her two-story house and bought one which had only one floor. Discussing the change with her he remarked that he preferred the two-story home. Immediately thereafter he got an attack in which he had to ask himself *questions about stories.* It was impossible at the time to understand the full meaning of the attack. Only now, in the latest phase of his analysis, had it become possible. He said that stories meant to him not only fairy tales, lies, but also floors in a building. At that point an old cynical joke came to my mind: "What is a kiss? An inquiry on the second floor whether the first is free." He had been happy to have solved the problem of mother's sex (breasts equal penis moved upward) and now she had only *one* story, the lower floor.

There is still another meaning attached to "stories." Stories are lies, as he said. Mother lied much to him, particularly in matters of sexuality. He was a keen observer and noticed that her tongue was rough as if it had holes, while his own and his sister's were smooth and pink. Mother would tell the children that they would bite their tongues if they told a lie. It was true that he was afraid to lie, but if occasionally he lied nevertheless, he wondered whether he did not bite holes in his tongue. Speculating about the "holes" in mother's tongue, he came to the conclusion that they must have been caused by father's penis, which seemed to him sharp as a knife. If he lied, he had a hole in his tongue like mother. That would mean that he was a woman; but he had no holes in his tongue, therefore it was not true that he was a woman, just as it was not true that mother had "bought him at Macy's" and would send him back if he was naughty.

When he was a very young child, his mother had her teeth pulled.[9] When he came into her bedroom in the morning and saw her false teeth in a glass beside her bed, he was puzzled. He pondered over it and finally found the explanation that father had knocked them out at night with his penis.

In an uninterrupted flow of associations he talked about his oral pregnancy and birth fantasies, as if he were connecting them with the parents' supposed oral activities at night. He added that when he learned later about homo-

[9] This happened at the time when it was fashionable to pull teeth in order to remove the source of focal infection allegedly causing schizophrenia and other psychic disorders. His mother was indeed very neurotic.

sexuality, he thought with horror that sexual intercourse between men might be performed orally. Out of the same horror, he said, he could not tell me that the woman whom he had observed through the window of the neighboring apartment was performing fellatio on the man. Immediately, however, he corrected himself, saying that he had not really seen the act, but that he had the impression that it was being performed, that in fact he imagined it afterward. The present attack had set in with the fear of the woman watching him while drinking. He imagined that in watching him she would be able to read his mind and discover that he had pleasure from drinking. *Actually, he was afraid that I would read his mind when I was watching him on the couch, that is, that I would detect his oral homosexual fantasies.*

As we remember, mother threatened him with (symbolic) castration when she caught him sucking his thumb. It was, however, extremely difficult for him to desist from it altogether; thumb sucking was his greatest pleasure. In order to prevent mother from watching him, he gave it up in daytime, but at night he covered his head with his blanket and indulged in thumb sucking and the accompanying fantasies. Most of his thinking and speculating took place

[55]

under the blanket. He kept these thoughts a well-guarded secret and constantly feared betraying them. In the course of his analysis he became afraid that I would detect his secrets, that is, his desires, fantasies, thoughts, and speculations. As he felt that most of them were wrong, forbidden, they had to be hidden. His fear of being looked at, specifically, included the fear of being caught at some wrongdoing. In order to protect himself from self-betrayal he developed a certain watchfulness which expressed itself in many traits, particularly in his cautious manner of talking, weighing every word carefully.

We are not surprised to learn that his questions about stories had still another connotation which fits perfectly in the mosaic of his thoughts. A storyteller meant to him a liar. He associated the word "lawyer" with the word "liar." From about his tenth to his nineteenth year he wanted to become a lawyer in order to defend criminals. In his fantasies, however, he did not see himself as a lawyer defending his client, but he saw himself in the courtroom, at one time as the prosecutor, another time as the defendant, thus *as the accuser and the accused.* As prosecutor he fired tormenting questions at the accused, i.e., at himself.

The problem of crime and punishment became ever more important to him; he spent much time speculating about it; he asked himself also whether he would hit his father back if he were hit by him, and whether he had the right to defend himself. At times he wished to have a gun for defending himself—from whom, he did not know.

Just as he felt crushed by the prosecutor's questioning in his courtroom fantasies, so he felt crushed and punished by the questions that he asked himself in his attacks. Many times he asked me why it was that he addressed himself in the second person, as, for instance, when he questioned himself, "Are there times when *you* tell stories . . ." There is no doubt—and he stressed this often—that he was punishing himself in these attacks. With this meaning of "stories" (lies) the circle seems almost closed. It is obvious that we have to do here with the relationship of the superego to the ego and the id.

The last attack began with fear of the woman who would by watching him discover that he derived pleasure from drinking. We have learned that he was actually afraid of my discovering his oral homosexual inclination. It was true, he remarked, that he considered this, as well as many of his other thoughts and wishes, highly immoral and was critical of them. But he could not understand why he was so afraid of me since nobody could possibly be more severely critical of him than he was himself.

His fear of being criticized was, of course, a manifestation of his conscience, of the fear of his superego, of which his analyst had become the representative in the outside world.

His first dream after the attack had a connection with this theme. There was a party where everything was confused, men were kissing women as well as men, everybody was kissing everybody else. Finally, he felt a *shadow* behind him, watching him. He awoke with anxiety. When he thought about this dream he was impressed by the "picture" of girls kissing girls and boys kissing boys as small children do who are not yet aware of the difference of sexes. Everybody loves everybody; they are free to love whomever they want. One of his obsessive questions at the beginning of the analysis was, as will be remembered, "Do I love people?" To which he answered, "Everybody loves everybody to a degree." At that time he was tormented by the question whether he loved men but did not have the courage to tell this to me. It was only now that he gave this supplementary information. Indeed, this time he came into analysis to talk freely about his homosexuality, which he considered a crime.

His fear of homosexuality was already so strong in his late high-school years that he was constantly on guard against an attack. He suspected teachers and schoolmates of the intention of seducing him; several times while walking in the street he had the feeling of being followed by a man and ran away in panic.[10] This fear that resembled a persecution mania was transitory and disappeared completely, while the fear of being looked at and investigated remained with him. The repetitive childhood dream of the man who searched for him with a flashlight is in a sense its precursor. He ran from the man to his sister as if looking for protection by her and, in a deeper layer, by the mother.[11] We shall refrain from going deeper into the topic of his homosexuality and return to the patient's curiosity, that is, to his questions.

[10] It happens in the course of the treatment that patients recollect such paranoid ideas or episodes, and sometimes such ideas enter the transference situation, making the analysis temporarily very difficult. But if there are no other signs of paranoia, they disappear sooner or later.

[11] It is not a rare occurrence that a man looks to the woman for protection from his homosexuality.

When he was covered with his blanket, sucking his thumb and speculating about his mother's womb (he always used the word "stomach"), he was particularly disturbed by two problems: how are babies fed there and how do they get in? The question how they escape from there did not bother him at that time; he had found an answer to it in his anal-birth theory, which, by the way, he had abandoned before the trip to Europe.

The solution of the puzzle how the babies get into the woman's "stomach" was determined by his unconscious symbolic equation "thumb-breast-penis": the woman swallows the penis, and children grow out of it in her stomach. Another idea coexisted with this one: not only girls but boys also can have babies, and consequently, he fantasied, he had babies in his stomach. In fact, he identified with women, specifically with his mother. This identification played an important role in his attacks of panic.

When he entered mother's bedroom in the morning, he would find her in bed feeling ill and miserable, complaining of headaches, dizziness, and nausea. He held his father responsible for her misery, and the sight of her in such a pitiful state increased his hate for him and aroused his compassion for her. Compassion means suffering with another one, that is, identifying with him in so far as she or he is suffering. The identification with mother became particularly evident in two situations: in his attacks of seasickness on the trip to Europe, and, as mentioned before, in the attacks of panic which set in when his questions and answers failed to satisfy him.

His was such a severe case of seasickness that everybody—stewards and passengers alike—was amazed that a child as young as he was could suffer so much from this illness. He had headaches, was dizzy, nauseous, and he vomited. He covered himself overhead with a blanket and kept away from everyone except his mother, whom he permitted to comfort him.[12] The symptoms in his attacks of panic were similar,

[12] I do not wish to imply here that the cause of seasickness is exclusively a mental one. However, it should be mentioned that before the trip he suffered from car sickness; when he was riding in the car with his parents, father and mother used to sit in front while he was in the back seat. After a while he became nauseated and began to vomit, whereupon the mother moved to the back seat, took his head in her lap and stroked and comforted him. He became peaceful and happy and fell asleep in a state of bliss. One might say he formed almost a unity with his mother, a complete identification.

The identification with the mother was different from the one with the father; it took place in the ego rather than in the superego as the latter did. The first was more of a libidinal, the second more of an aggressive character.

indeed almost identical: headache, dizziness, nausea, vomiting, seclusion in his bedroom, shades drawn and lights out. Thus the seasickness and the attacks of panic reflected the condition in which he would find his mother when he entered her bedroom in the morning. It can hardly be doubted that he identified with her in the situation of suffering. As was pointed out, he imagined that his father had knocked out her teeth (castrated her), cut her, and forced her to swallow his penis. Thus he was dramatizing or acting out on himself what he imagined the father had done to his mother. Often in later life he complained that his attacks were tortures and punishments inflicted upon him.

But what has that to do with looking, investigating, questioning—in brief, with curiosity?

The first answer is that his attacks of panic set in when he could not find a satisfactory answer to one of his questions; that is, when his curiosity was frustrated. Secondly, it struck him that there was a difference in his reaction to the sight of each parent in nudity. He remembered clearly seeing his mother as she went about undressed in her bedroom, or as she sat in the bathtub. He did not feel ashamed or embarrassed. On the contrary, he liked to look at her, especially at her breasts.[13] But he could not remember having seen his father naked, although he must have on many occasions—in the bathroom, in locker and shower rooms, and in solaria where the father used to take him. Although all the men in these places, his father included, were naked, he himself put a towel around his hips. The adults tried to persuade him to remove the towel, they ridiculed him, but to no avail. On the one hand, he was afraid to look at his father's nudity; on the other, he was afraid to be looked at when naked. His fear of being looked at by men derives from fear of retaliation, that is, castration by the father for looking at him with aggressive intentions. In other words, he feared that his father would do to him what he himself wished to do to the father. (The Biblical legend of Noah comes to mind who cursed his son when he became aware that the latter had looked at his nudity.) But where is the link with orality? The patient *maintained that when one sees something desirable, one wants to have, to eat it,* just as he felt that his sister wanted to have his penis, to bite

[13] Obviously this recollection refers to early childhood, not to latency or later years, for in these periods he would look surreptitiously at his mother while she was dressing or undressing, and as a mature man he became embarrassed when she dressed in his presence.

[63]

it off, when she *"looked at me with her greedy eyes."* But this is not sufficient to explain the relationship between the castration complex and orality.

Let me insert another detail here. When his mother urged him to drink milk, she would ask, "Do you not want to be as strong and tall as your father?" Certainly he always wanted to be as big and powerful as his father; but whenever he forced himself to drink milk, he was obsessed by thoughts about milking cows and squeezing their teats, and about playing with mother's breasts. In the transference situation he became aware that he had also wished to suck his father's penis (Nunberg, 1936). However, he hesitated for a long time to convey this idea to the analyst because it was unbearable to him. Moreover, in the unconscious a part stands for the whole; therefore swallowing the penis must have meant swallowing the whole father —an even more horrifying idea.

As you know, it is assumed that in prehistoric times the primeval father was killed by his sons and incorporated in an oral (cannibalistic) act, and that later, in further development, this physical act became a psychic one, which is called identification. Through this specific identification the superego develops, which is, in a sense, the psychic representation of the father in the ego and exercises a moral influence on the individual. If it functions properly, the individual in the course of development becomes gradually less dependent on the father's judgment than on the superego's.[14]

Alerted by this fragment of theory we can almost see how from the chaotic, unorganized mental life of the little child our patient's moral personality emerged. As a child he was afraid of his father in the external world; later on this fear decreased while the fear of and dependence on his superego increased. In the transference situation he was afraid that the analyst might know what he tried to hide, that he would know and see his homosexual and aggressive wishes toward the analyst. Thus he projected his superego onto the analyst. Since the latter was a substitute for the father—as is regularly the case in treatment—the patient re-established in this way the original situation where he was afraid of his father's omniscience. In his fear of being looked at by the father he projected onto him his own curiosity and aggression. Since the superego develops, as we have just recapitulated, by means of identification

[14] See Freud, *Totem and Taboo* (1913), *The Ego and the Id* (1923), and other works.

which is a derivative of oral incorporation and
since it acts as a critical inner eye, we may assume that it stems not only from auditive im-
pressions but also from visual ones. It is as if
by consuming the father, the son acquired the
omniscience the father of his childhood pos-
sessed. And what he wanted to know in childhood was what father was doing with mother.
In other words, through identification with
father he would acquire father's knowledge and
be able to do with mother what father did.

Incidentally, we may perhaps have found a
way to understand one aspect of the passage in
Genesis which tells us that Adam *knew* Eve
after he had eaten of the tree of knowledge. If
we assume, as Theodor Reik (1957) does that
the tree of knowledge represents a totem
(father) god, the meaning of the myth would be
that Adam, having swallowed the father (god)
and identified with him, acquired his knowledge, i.e., sexual *knowledge*.[15] We know, indeed,
from our analyses how fervently boys desire to

[15] I owe to Mr. Gerson Cohen of the New York Jewish Theo-
logical Seminary the following information. The Hebrew word
yada means "to know," *lamad* means "to learn, to study." Only
yada is used in the sexual sense; the basic meaning of both words
is "experience." In the Ugaritic epic *Gilgamesh* the hero Enkidu
becomes wise (i.e., has gained knowledge) and therefore like the
gods, only after a sexual experience.

be introduced to the mysteries of sex by their *fathers*. In other words, one can have sexual relations with mother when one acquires the necessary knowledge through identification with father.

Let us now return to our patient. As we have seen, the thought of drinking milk and becoming as strong as father set in motion the entire chain of associations connected with oral agression against him. The aim of this oral aggressivity was, in a sense, fulfilled in the psychic incorporation of or identification with the father through which one becomes as tall, as strong, as omnipotent and omniscient as he is. The fusion of orality with scoptophilia may perhaps become more understandable if we think of the superego and its function, the conscience, as the result of incorporation. As you know, the word "conscience" stems from the Latin *co-scire*, which means to know together with. The German word *Gewissen* has the same literal meaning. Theodor Reik reminds us that the word "remorse" is derived from the Latin *mordere*, which means "to bite"; its German counterpart is *Gewissensbisse*— which means "bites of conscience." Thus language gives us an almost pictorial presentation of the relationship between superego and ego, as if indicating: the superego "watches and bites" the ego.

After theoretical speculations it is advisable to direct one's attention again to reality. Our patient's sexual curiosity was beginning to subside before the trip to Europe. After his return home, however—he was then seven years old—his questions re-emerged. Yet it was no longer so much in speculations, fantasies, and theories that he tried to find answers to them as in actions. As we know, he had not only the fantasy that he, a boy, could have a baby, but he identified himself also with the fantasied unborn baby. At that time he thought that a baby is born by micturation; however, he did not adhere long to this theory because it seemed impossible to him that a baby could pass through the small urethral orifice; thus he resorted to his old fantasy that a baby is cut out of the mother's womb and concluded in analogy that his child would have to be cut out of his penis. Then another difficulty presented itself to him: would not penis and child be injured by the surgeon's knife? In order to resolve this problem he resorted to an experiment. Having seen the cook taking peas out of the pod he took a knife and cut a pod open. When he found that he could not cut the pod without scratching the peas, he stopped the experiment. From that day on he could eat neither peas nor any other food that had to be removed from a shell, such as nuts, oysters, and the like. He had, of course, identified with pea and pod. Nevertheless, this experiment implies a certain progress; with it he took one step closer to reality. Up to that point he had only speculated and fantasied, now he projected his ideas and fantasies into the outside world and experimented there, like a scientist. His castration fear, however, caused him to desist from further experimentation. Had his castration complex been less powerful he might perhaps have become a scientific explorer.

He became no scientist but an excellent business man. And although his infantile sexual curiosity did not bring him closer to reality, it sharpened his thinking processes. It stimulated the emergence of manifold problems which he endeavored to solve by complicated reasoning, by speculations, which in a sense, provided a preparatory training for his future logical thinking. Naturally, as long as his questions were dominated by the sexual instinct, his answers were wrapped in "theories" and fantasies, far removed from reality. Only when his curiosity gradually was cleared of the sexual admixture did better reality testing and logical thinking begin to evolve. His attempt to find an answer to his questions in the pea-pod experiment was a manifestation of an intermediary period in which he projected his fantasies into the external world and looked there for an answer to his tormenting questions instead of within himself. An example of the progressive development of his reality testing and logical thinking is afforded by his behavior after the return from Europe. We recall that he decided to take up athletics in order to become manly and thereby to please his father; before every contest he practiced very hard and calculated every step of the game in advance, be it baseball, golf, or any other sport, so that not a single move was left to chance. No wonder that he became a champion and earned many trophies. He wanted to become a man like father, and we know that identification with the father facilitates adaptation to reality considerably. Goethe's words come to mind:

> Vom Vater hab' ich die Statur,
> Des Lebens ernstes Führen,
> Vom Mütterchen die Frohnatur
> Und Lust zu fabulieren.

[From Father I have looks and build
And the serious conduct of living;
My mother gave me gaiety
And zest for spinning stories.]

The patient's attempts to solve sexual-aggressive problems evidently helped him in later life to solve problems in general, problems of a practical nature. He always carried a notebook in his pocket in which he used to jot down all the questions he could not solve immediately. When he entered his father's business he continued this habit, now in relation to the business. In an almost scientific manner he set up teams for investigating certain problems for which he had no explanation, and when his father retired, he reorganized the business, using the information gained in the course of these investigations. Gradually he succeeded in making his company one of the largest and most prosperous of its kind in the country. This man who never studied mechanical engineering was called upon for help by the factory manager, a trained engineer, when some machine was out of order and nobody was able to repair it. He would work there—sometimes for weeks— until he found the cause of failure, which his trained men had not been able to detect.

These few examples show how the infantile

sexual curiosity lost the sexual component during the course of development and turned from
fantasy to the solution of real problems. In
other words, the infantile sexual curiosity was
sublimated and paved the way for adaptation to
reality.[16]

As stated at the beginning of this paper, all
human beings are equipped with a certain
amount of curiosity. It seems that its first manifestations appear in earliest childhood. Our
patient's first dream tends to support the as-
sumption that curiosity is already active in the
primal scene when the infant wants to know
what the parents are doing together. Of course,
that wish cannot be conscious since the child

[16] The adaptation to reality is a very complex problem. Here
is not the place to discuss it in detail; however, I would like to
take this opportunity to correct a misunderstanding which is
expressed in Dr. R. Lowenstein's paper on Masochism (1957, p.
211). He writes: "Hartmann refutes the theory advanced by
Ferenczi (29) and taken over by Nunberg (76) according to which
all adjustment to reality is based on masochism. He thinks the
latter may be found in cases of psychoses (Nunberg) or may exist
when reality is painful, but certainly not in adjustment to any
kind of reality."

I do not understand how the authors arrived at this conclusion
about my view on adaptation to reality. In my book, *Principles
of Psychoanalysis* (1955; German edition, 1932, under the title,
Allgemeine Neurosenlehre), to which the authors refer I stated
that we have to distinguish between passive and active adaptation to reality and that passive adaptation is only an intermediary stage which is followed by active adaptation. Without
active participation there is no effective adaptation to reality.

has no ability nor facility to formulate a question. Since a primal scene may or may not have occurred, we have reason to believe that curiosity arises independently. It seems, indeed, to set in shortly after birth. For the observer gets the impression that the suckling is searching for the erotogenic zones of his body. First it is the mouth which the baby tries to reach with his hands. As soon as he has found it, he puts his fingers in and sucks them with ecstatic pleasure. But he does not stop here in his explorations; he continues to search for other erotogenic zones. Unmistakable is the pleasure when he detects parts of his body, such as hands, toes, or earlobes. Finally he discovers the genital zone. It looks as if the child were born with a kind of instinct to investigate. Freud calls curiosity at times an instinct of investigation; at other times he says that such an instinct does not exist. Since curiosity manifests itself so early and with such urgency, it seems difficult to deny that it at least behaves like the derivative of an instinct. Anyway, it is clear that curiosity, in its earliest stages, is amalgamated with sexuality. In the course of development it loses its sexual component and, if we take into account the indefatigable compulsion to repeat inherent in curiosity, we cannot but agree with Freud that one of its

[73]

functions is to help in mastering the external world, the reality. In the need for mastery we see a derivative of the aggressive instincts; indeed, infantile curiosity contains much aggression fused with the sexual instinct.

Infantile sexual curiosity is concerned mainly with three questions: where do children come from; what is the difference between a boy and a girl; and what are father and mother doing together? Usually answers to these questions are provided by the children themselves in the typical fantasies.

In our patient, however, the problems of conception and birth seem gradually to have pushed into the background all the other sexual questions. They persisted longer than the others and absorbed a great amount of psychic energy.

Although in normal development sexual curiosity can be mastered by the ego and inhibited to a high degree, in truth it cannot be suppressed completely. Everybody knows what role it plays in normal love life.

The question about the origin of man occupies not only the mind of the individual child but it has occupied mankind from primeval times onward. In most religions men projected the solution of this problem onto their gods, leaving to them the task of creating the first

[74]

man. According to the Biblical myth, God blew life into a piece of earth, thus creating Adam. In all mythologies earth is a symbol for the mother (Mother Earth). If we substitute "mother" for "earth" in the creation myth, we see that it has great similarity to one of our patient's fantasies about the birth of a child. Why birth had to be represented in a disguised and desexualized form in most of the creation myths, is a problem which does not belong in our context.

Originally, the patient asked what or who caused the child to be born; later on, why the machine in his factory stopped functioning or why some products were selling better than others, etc. When he found the cause, he knew how to put the machine back into function or how to improve his business. A child tries to find out not only what the cause of an event is but also who creates the cause, rather who is the cause. Just as in childhood man feels compelled to fantasy about his origin, so he feels compelled in a more advanced stage of his development to think about the cause of some phenomena. From the phenomenological point of view causal thinking seems to be the manifestation of a need to connect two phenomena in such a manner that the second is determined by the first. This need is called the *need for causality*.

I am not talking here about causality as a philosophical problem but about the *need* for causality, a psychological phenomenon. Everyone feels it as a wish to find, to establish the relationship between cause and effect. It is a deeply rooted need; it is known that the younger or the more primitive an individual is, the more easily he will find causal connections. To the primitive man or the little child, everything in the world around him seems animated and has its creator.

When the child sees a newborn baby he senses that the parents have something to do with his appearance; i.e., that a man and a woman do something with one another and the result is a new human being. All of this stimulates his curiosity. In a paper written a long time ago (1930) I derived the need for causality from this infantile sexual curiosity. It needed but one step further to recognize that the synthetic function of the ego stems from the same source. Its most comprehensive task is binding, unifying. This conception is based on Freud's instinct theory.[17] As you know, he distinguishes two groups of instincts: the sexual or erotic and the aggressive

[17] See Freud, *Beyond the Pleasure Principle* (1920).

or destructive instincts. The interaction of these two instinct groups reveals itself in the phenomenon which we call life. The sexual instincts or Eros have the tendency to bring two individuals together and to join them in the act of love. When this libidinal instinct of the id enters the ego and is discharged in sexual union, a child is born. If it enters the ego and is not discharged in the sexual act, it loses its sexual character but retains the binding, unifying, creative quality of Eros, though on a higher level. It permeates the ego and appears as its synthetic function. Because of its derivation from Eros the synthetic function comprises also the creative faculty of the ego, just as the need for causality comprises the need to understand the phenomena of life and nature in general. If one understands a phenomenon one may perhaps be able to recreate it. That may be the meaning of Freud's statement that curiosity serves the purpose of mastering reality.

The original sexual curiosity of the child confronts him with a variety of problems that he tries to solve in his fantasies and "theories." In the attempt to solve similar problems mankind in its infancy resorted to the creation myths. In further development man searched for the elixir of life, for the stone of wisdom.

Paracelsus and his followers expected to create the *homunculus* in the test tube; Darwin postulated his theory of evolution; and in our times man tries to penetrate the secrets of matter.

Curiosity and the need for causality are boundless. There are individuals whose urge to know is unlimited and whose ego seems to lose control over this urge and to become its prisoner. Individuals of this type may be utterly ruthless in their avidity for knowledge and totally unconcerned with the possible consequences of their search. They may not even be deterred by the prospect of comprehensive destruction, including their own, when they hope to come closer to their goal. One gets the impression that the pure instinct of destruction has been released in them. Indeed, Freud says that with sublimation there occurs not only desexualization but at the same time a defusion of the two groups of instincts which sets destructive instincts free. Since infantile sexual curiosity as such contains an aggressive element, we might say that the explorer, in a sense, returns to the level of the child who ruthlessly tries to satisfy his curiosity.

Curiosity may, on the one hand, be a blessing and stimulate intellectual performances of the highest value; on the other hand, it may lead to destruction if too much aggression is released. We may, perhaps, take comfort from the observation that nature often enhances the creative and constructive forces when excessive destructive power has been freed.

References

Freud, Anna (1936), *The Ego and the Mechanisms of Defense.* New York: International Universities Press, 1946.

Freud, Sigmund (1905), Three Essays on the Theory of Sexuality. *Standard Edition, 7*:125-245. London: Hogarth Press, 1953.

—— (1908), Character and Anal Erotism. *Standard Edition, 9*:167-176. London: Hogarth Press, 1959.

—— (1910), Leonardo da Vinci and a Memory of His Childhood. *Standard Edition, 11*:59-137. London: Hogarth Press, 1957.

—— (1913), *Totem and Taboo. Standard Edition, 13*:1-162. London: Hogarth Press, 1955.

—— (1920), Beyond the Pleasure Principle. *Standard Edition, 18*:7-64. London: Hogarth Press, 1955.

—— (1921), Group Psychology and the Analysis of the Ego. *Standard Edition, 18*:67-143. London: Hogarth Press, 1955.

—— (1923), *The Ego and the Id.* London: Hogarth Press, 1948.

Loewenstein, R. M. (1957), A Contribution to the Psychoanalytic Theory of Masochism. *Journal of the American Psychoanalytic Association, 5*:197-234.

[81]

REFERENCES

Nunberg, Herman (1925), The Will to Recovery. *Practice and Theory of Psychoanalysis*. New York: International Universities Press, 1961, pp. 75-88.

—— (1930), The Synthetic Function of the Ego. *Practice and Theory of Psychoanalysis*. New York: International Universities Press, 1961, pp. 120-136.

—— (1932), *Allgemeine Neurosenlehre auf psychoanalytischer Grundlage*. Bern: Hans Huber, 2nd ed., 1959.

—— (1936), Homosexuality, Magic and Aggression. *Practice and Theory of Psychoanalysis*. New York: International Universities Press, 1961, pp. 150-164.

—— (1947), *Problems of Bisexuality As Reflected in Circumcision*. London: Imago Publishing Co., 1949.

—— (1951), Transference and Reality. *International Journal of Psycho-Analysis, 32*:1-9.

—— (1955), *Principles of Psychoanalysis*. New York: International Universities Press.

Rank, Otto (1913), Totemismus im Märchen; Rv Grimmschen Märchen. *Imago, 2*:594-596.

Reik, Theodor (1957), *Myth and Guilt*. New York: George Braziller.

Publications by Dr. Nunberg

1910

Körperliche Begleiterscheinungen assoziativer Vorgänge. *J. Psychol. Neurol.* Also in *Diagnostische Assoziationsstudien,* ed. C. G. Jung. Leipzig: Barth, 1914.

1913

Niespelnione Zyczenia wedlug nanki Freuda [The Unfulfilled Wishes According to Freud's Teachings]. *Neurologia Polska,* 3 (Jan.-Feb.).

1920

Über den katatonen Anfall. *Int. Ztschr. Psa.,* 6:25-49
  English: On the Catatonic Attack. Chap. I in *Practice and Theory of Psychoanalysis*

1921

Der Verlauf des Libidokonfliktes in einem Falle von Schizophrenie. *Int. Ztschr. Psa.,* 7:301-345
  English: The Course of the Libidinal Conflict in a Case of Schizophrenia. Chap. II in *Practice and Theory of Psychoanalysis*

1924

Über Depersonalisationszustände im Lichte der Libidotheorie. *Int. Ztschr. Psa.*, 10:17-33

English: States of Depersonalization in the Light of the Libido Theory. Chap. III in *Practice and Theory of Psychoanalysis*

1925

Über den Genesungswunsch. *Int. Ztschr. Psa.*, 11:179-193

English: The Will to Recovery. *Int. J. Psa.*, 7:64-78, 1926; also Chap. IV in *Practice and Theory of Psychoanalysis*

1926

Schuldgefühl und Strafbedürfnis. *Int. Ztschr. Psa.*, 12:348-359

English: The Sense of Guilt and the Need for Punishment. *Int. J. Psa.*, 7:420-433, 1926; also Chap. V in *Practice and Theory of Psychoanalysis*

Ein Traum eines sechsjährigen Mädchens. *Ztschr. psa. Päd.*, 1:22-24, 1926-27

English: A Dream of a Six-Year-Old Girl. Chap. VI in *Practice and Theory of Psychoanalysis*

Über den Traum. *Das psychoanalytische Volksbuch*, ed. Paul Federn & Heinrich Meng. Bern: Hans Huber, pp. 75-90; 1928, 1:82-99; 1939, 88-101

1927

Diskussion der Laienanalyse. *Int. Ztschr. Psa.*, 13:306-307

English: Discussion of Lay Analysis. *Int. J. Psa.*, 8:247-248, 1927

1928

Probleme der Therapie. *Int. Ztschr. Psa.*, 14:441-457
English: Problems of Therapy. Chap. VII in *Practice and Theory of Psychoanalysis*; also in *The Yearbook of Psychoanalysis*, 5:35-50. New York: International Universities Press, 1949

1930

Die synthetische Funktion des Ich. *Int. Ztschr. Psa.*, 16:301-318
English: The Synthetic Function of the Ego. *Int. J. Psa.*, 12:123-140, 1931; also Chap. VIII in *Practice and Theory of Psychoanalysis*

1932

Allgemeine Neurosenlehre auf psychoanalytischer Grundlage. Geleitwort von Sigm. Freud. Bern: Hans Huber; 2nd ed., 1959
English (expanded): see 1955
Deckerinnerungen an ein Spiel. *Ztschr. psa. Päd.*, 6:263-264
Psychoanalyse des Schamgefühls. *Psa. Bewegung,* 4:505-507

1933

Theoretical Basis of Psychoanalytic Therapy. *Psychoanalysis Today.* New York: Covici-Friede
Magie und Allmacht. *Almanach der Psa.*, 88-95

1934

Das Schuldgefühl. *Imago,* 20:257-268
English: The Feeling of Guilt. *Psa. Quart.*, 3:589-604, 1934; also Chap. IX in *Practice and Theory of Psychoanalysis*

[85]

1936

Homosexualität, Magie und Aggression. *Int. Ztschr. Psa.*, 22:5-18

English: Homosexuality, Magic and Aggression. *Int. J. Psa.*, 19:1-16, 1938; also Chap. X in *Practice and Theory of Psychoanalysis*

1937

The Theory of the Therapeutic Results of Psychoanalysis. *Int. J. Psa.*, 18:161-169; also Chap. XI in *Practice and Theory of Psychoanalysis*

Beiträge zur Theorie der Therapie. *Int. Ztschr. Psa.*, 23:60-67

1938

Psychological Interrelations between Physician and Patient. *Psa. Rev.*, 25:297-308; also Chap. XII in *Practice and Theory of Psychoanalysis*

Spanish: Interrelación psicológia entre médico y paciente. *Rev. Psicoanál.*, 8:430-439, 1951

1939

Ichstärke und Ichschwäche. *Int. Ztschr. Psa.*, 24:49-61

English: Ego Strength and Ego Weakness, *Am. Imago*, 3:25-40, 1942; also Chap. XIII in *Practice and Theory of Psychoanalysis*

1943

Limitations of Psychoanalytic Treatment. *J. Nerv. & Ment. Dis.*, 97:469-474; also in *Bull. N.Y. Acad. Med.*, 19:729-738, 1943; *Arch. Neurol. Psychiat.*, 50:98-100, 1943; and Chap. XIV in *Practice and Theory of Psychoanalysis*

[86]

1947

Circumcision and Problems of Bisexuality. *Int. J. Psa.*, 28:145-179. Reprinted under title: *Problems of Bisexuality As Reflected in Circumcision*. London: Imago Publishing Co., 1949

Spanish: La circuncisión y los problemas de la bisexualidad. *Rev. Psicoanál.*, 9:55-122, 1952

1948

Practice and Theory of Psychoanalysis. A Collection of Essays. New York: Nervous and Mental Disease Monographs No. 74; 2nd ed., New York: International Universities Press, 1961

1950

A Commentary on Freud's *An Outline of Psychoanalysis*. *Psa. Quart.*, 19:227-250; also in *The Yearbook of Psychoanalysis*, 7:9-30. New York: International Universities Press, 1951

1951

Transference and Reality. *Int. J. Psa.*, 32:1-9

1952

Discussion of M. Katan's paper on Schreber's Hallucination. *Int. J. Psa.*, 33:454-456

1954

Evaluation of the Results of Psycho-Analytic Treatment. *Int. J. Psa.*, 35:2-7

1955

Principles of Psychoanalysis. New York: International Universities Press

Spanish: *Teoría general de las neurosis basada en el psicoanálisis.* Barcelona: Editorial Pupul, 1950
French: *Principes de psychanalyse; leur application aux neuroses.* Paris: Presses Universitaires de France, 1957

1961

Introduction and footnotes to *Minutes of the Vienna Psychoanalytic Society.* New York: International Universities Press (in print)